REFLECTIONS ON THE DARK WATER

poems by **M. P. Jones**

Solomon and George Publishers
108 S 8th Street
Opelika, AL 36801

Copyright 2016
ALL RIGHTS RESERVED

No part of this work may be reproduced or transmitted in any form or by any means, whether electronic or mechanical, including photocopying and recording, or by any infomation storage or retrieval system without the proper written permission of the copright owner.

1. Poetry 2. Environment 3. The American South

ISBN: 978-0-9966839-1-3

First Edition

Cover image by Lynn Sears

Cover design by Iris Saya Miller

For Jane

Contents

The Bicycle   2

I.

Fish Tale   5
Ubi Sunt   7
The Broken Branch   8
Passenger   10
Morning Otology   11
A Genealogy of Silence   13
A Heron   15
Bone-Music Sutra   16
To the Liquor Store with Hayden Carruth   18
Recycling   19
Self-Portrait as Silent Ritual   20
Emily Dickinson Sewed Her Poems Shut   22
Plastic Realms   23
Funeral Games   24
Threshing Floor   25
Against Naming the Dead   26

II.

Amphora   29
The Burden of Dumah   32
At the Planer   34
A Note from the Edomites   35
Nero Bathes in the Aqua Marcia   36
Prayer for the Great Dog, Central Alabama   37
Incantation   38
Jim Morrison Believed That the Right Words
   in the Right Order Could Kill You   39
I Am Singing Now as Rome Burns   40

Self-Portrait as Apollo and Dionysus 41
The Silent Thrush 42
Throughout the Dismal Glade Our Bodies
  Shall Be Hung, Each on the Wild Thorn
of His Wretched Shade 43
A Mill at Sunset 44

III.

Middle of Nowhere, Five-Thirty 47
Break of Dawn 48
Nostos 49
Red Sky at Morning 50
Field Grief 51
One-Man Renga in Late June, Lee County 52
Fig Tree 54
Roundel on a Thursday Morning 55
Self-Portrait at the Mouth of Summer 56
Sunfall Triolet 58
The Campfire 59
Nocturne in an Empty Field 60
At Six, I Prayed for Snow in Alabama 61
Self-Portrait in a Broken Mirror 62
Rain Follows the Plow 64
Night Rendering 65
Futurist Author Egotists 67
Coyote Makes This World 68
Blackberry Winter 71

Notes 72
Acknowledgements 73
About the Author 77

"The past becomes such a mirror—we're in it, and then we're not"

—Charles Wright

The Bicycle

Almost nothing separates this tiny boat
from gathering silence and darkness
pooling along the starless cow fields
abandoned as the pine shack that fell
in forgotten woods of youth. No division
between the deep taproots and the loam,
nothing to displace the topography of ruin
save for my panting and the whirring
of feet, of shoes clipped to pedals,
of the gears, of the wheels, of the tires,
of the desolate road, the empty night.

I

Fish Tale

My brother died with a trunk full of fish
               and beer bottles crashing together—
                           in the Mother's Day darkness—
I am endlessly returning
                     as if to a worn photograph,
a lure drifting along the lake's rim
                           in Vermont,
a place I've never seen, and so
can only imagine some dim shore growing certain
          in torn threads of afternoon light.
I go back to those improbable stories

he would tell, eyes alight with the consuming
fire of beer and bourbon,

like the one where he is driving through the desert
all night,
just driving through the sand, until finally he stops
at noon—perhaps in Arizona,
                          perhaps nowhere at all—

on a waterless sea of solid glass,
supposedly the wake of some explosives test.

Walking over the burnt sand-lake's surface, breaking apart
                     frozen waves and currents
beneath his boots,
crumbling like some hopeless metaphor for certainty.

I listen as he wavers—wanting only to fix some narrative
over the near end—
                          recounting as his slurring sways,
circling to the moment just before the hooks are set,

before the surface quivers,
the bottles break,
          and everything is finished.

And everything *is* finished:
                          the bottles break
            before the surface quivers,

circling to the moment just before the hooks are set,
            recounting as his slurring sways

                                      over the near end,
I listen as he wavers, wanting only to fix some narrative.

Crumbling. Like some hopeless metaphor for certainty
beneath his boots,
            frozen waves and currents.

Walking over the burnt sand-lake's surface, breaking apart—
            supposedly the wake of some explosives test—

                      on a waterless sea of solid glass.
Perhaps nowhere at all
            at noon, perhaps in Arizona,
just driving through the sand, until finally he stops
all night.

Like the one where he is driving through the desert
                      fire of beer and bourbon.

He would tell, eyes alight with the consuming.

I go back to those improbable stories
            in torn threads of afternoon light,

can only imagine some dim shore growing certain—
            a place I've never seen—and so,

in Vermont,
            a lure drifting along the lake's rim
as if to a worn photograph—
            I am endlessly returning
in the Mother's day darkness
            and beer bottles crashing together.
My brother died with a trunk full of fish.

Ubi Sunt

The monarchs have not been seen
for years in the numbers
with which they burst
over the washout
where we built our garden
when we had all the strength of our youth
and worked the ruined earth
like blue music
drifting over the cold riverwater,
resting on the cucumber's soft leaves,
and there fluttered
like dawnlight over the high hill,
borrowing their heat
from our summer air,
rising up over the dark river
until they vanished behind the bridge,
and then where did they go?

The Broken Branch
after James Wright

Standing on the stone path
before the cabin door, staring out
at the scarred oak that leaned
in the dooryard, ancient and solemn,
shading the cedar fence and the fire pit
where we gathered until late,
when the stars echoed their bright
syllables across the pasture.

By the time the first branch has fallen
onto the soft loam outside
the windows of the empty house
in the cold afternoon light,
the trunk is already hollow,
mute, illiterate, nearly forgotten
as it strangles with dirt
from the steady motion
of the carpenter ants,

the deliberate sunlight
pressing against everything
like a miller's wheel,
turning drops of shadow
violently from the hole,
dripping tiny fragments of dark earth
where the black branch hung,
sorrowful and late,
until the orange heart
crumbled to dirt and ruin.

Those owls who nested there
all those long winters would haunt
the deepest nights with songs
of their longing. When the mother
leapt from branch to branch,
crying out as her fledglings left,
leaping one-by-one into the fieldgrass.

You would go, grandfather,
so faithfully to clear the debris
from the dying trunk, until your
own body lay in ruin. And the ice
storm came in the night, as I slept
alone in the dark house, with light
from dying embers licking the ceiling.

And the tree threatened, even in its ruin,
to survive you in the desolate field,
but it had grown so heavy
with the worn tenor of night,
like the edge of some long road
coming abruptly to its end
before you can even imagine
that it cannot begin to bear
the weight of its own memory
or offer its relentless green refuge.

And those owls who knew
not how to weep or were too wise
that nested there have long flown.

Passenger

Once the most common
bird, named from French, *passager*,
which means "passing by."

Morning Otology

Summer air condenses on the windows,
    rattled as if by cicada screech.

When I was twelve my father stood
        over the tires of an old scooter
we bought earlier that day
        at a neighbor's yard sale,

filling them with free air
        from the corner station
until the dry-rotted tires exploded from the pressure.

Now night's voice whispers
        out of the ruptured membrane
between this world and the sound of silence.

    The ringing ruined sex for Rousseau,

who heard it as death rattling
        his ears, so he wrote instead, scratching a pen
across the soft palette.

The neighbor passes again
        on the green mower.

        Emperor Titus thought a gnat
had crawled in a nostril
    to pick his brain as punishment

for destroying the Second Temple.
        No oracle could forestall the madness
of that constant sound,
        though they prescribed

Ibex tooth charms,

            wild cumin and almond oil,

abstinence from wine,

            opium and mandrake.

What is this space between
            spoken and unknown, this smoldering
peal tolling like petals on the tabletop.

Darwin heard the sonorous note
            when bedridden, suffering

a host of strange maladies
        which afforded him world enough
and sound to stave away

"distractions of society
            and amusement." When still,

locusts descend. Jaw swivel
            like altitudinous passengers
without chewing gum.

When it is spring, I miss
            the silence most, when it is summer,

when out morning windows,

song is in bloom.

A Genealogy of Silence

1917: An American boy and a German boy stare
at one another in a French trench for a full minute
behind a Colt New Service and a Luger.
Each marvels at how close a likeness the other
bears to his own visage, like a mirror image. One shoots.

1925: She watches the shadows swim under the door
as her impatient husband paces the hospital corridor.

1936: A man films the last known Tasmanian tiger
walking back and forth between the cage walls
just before it disappears.

1952: A soldier's hat falls as he bends to avoid seeing
his superior. Polished boots sound like hoof-clatter
on cobblestones as he slams the brothel door.

1970: In a soybean field in middle Georgia, the crowd roars.
Not far away, a pregnant girl at a roadside peach stand
says to a Strychnine-panicked boy, "I cannot help you;
the lines are down," as he stumbles into the darkness.

1976: A red telephone is ringing in the early light. She cannot
hear it. She studies the light on the countertop, not wondering
who waits at the other end of the line, for whom it rings.

1987: A girl waits in a hotel room purchased on her father's
credit card for a boy who said, "I ache for you."

1993: A man holds his first-born by the legs out the window-
frame of an incomplete second-story addition.

1997: A young man drives through the night, perhaps in
Arizona, perhaps nowhere at all, until he comes upon
a waterless sea of solid glass. Nobody believes him.

2000:   The neighbor boy soaks toads in gasoline to watch
          them move through the dark like shooting stars.

2004:   Christmas eve, the tire of an overturned car spins
          in a ditch where two boys sit staring at a patch
          of morning sun shining through the pines.

2005:   Midnight in the mother's day darkness:
          the telephone rings.

2012:   A young man cuts his own right hand off
          with a chainsaw. After, he cannot explain.

2013:   Forgotten candles in the bathroom resemble
          green moonlight where two lay naked in the dark.

Five   A boy and a girl watch the last Tasmanian tiger
(A.M.):   pace back and forth on a bright screen. No sound.

A Heron

Crossing the highway sky
like a blue comet streak,
halfway from where I stand
and the distant clouds
with the sun already
leaning into the dark,
a heron casts its frail
shadow into the long legged
summer afternoon
and disappears behind
the shortleaf horizon
sloping beyond the crest
of the hill and power lines
which rise and fall,
dipping further down
into the silent air,
and I am left
to imagine it moving
across this strange landscape
of strip malls and traffic,
perhaps seeking shelter
in the drainage lake
of the Briggs & Stratton
industrial park.

Bone-Music Sutra

Perhaps you've heard
this one before. We begin

as this moment
untangles skeins

of naked selves, pale light's
meager play in the hemlock.

We cannot mind
the silence of this day,

and only this one past,
an illusion like when

history swells, purple
as a broken nose,

until we scour the earth
beneath our fingernails

where silence gathers
and ears fill with shadow.

* * *

In the dooryard of my parents house,
where the dogwood once hung

and would flower
with such fervor and purpose,

the tree they planted the day
I was born. Now it is gone.

The ducks are bobbing
in the plastic pond.

Spring joggers bloom
and burn. The chestnut

rattles lost obituaries.
Wind in the gutter

slammed hours behind it
like a red door in a house

you never lived in. There is
no homecoming, except

nostalgia's silent resonance, wick
or wire, the weight of thought.

* * *

Noon song, shrill spring,
though it was written

somewhere in our bones,
we couldn't read it.

The stale shadows,
daylight's little wings.

So we wore the night
like a thriftstore dinner jacket,

sackcloth where it met skin,
unraveling at the seams

until it fit us best.

To the Liquor Store with Hayden Carruth

        Even at your age, you are as thirsty
as Li Po at sunset, picturing endless herons
           with the lake's *orange tongues leaping in the corner,*

so we make way, with *the winter of illness ending,*
        down main street,
               suffering through what was left

of that pitiful hangover, the dreadful *crescent tipped beyond*
the dark tree-burst of morning. The Oldsmobile

        that burns oil and rocks violently
like a *cat* that *starts to throw up,*
        back and forth, *convulsing and gagging—*

you think *Chicago was bleak, God knows,*
        but sweet, well, what is this cow town,
               anonymous as its barren azaleas,
before the students crawl out from beneath

their drowsy squalor? Hayden, you wince
        a devil grin as we take the corner sharply—
past where *Omar* and *Tu Fu* were *drinking vodka*

and warm beer—eyes glowing hellfire, you struggle
             like Ahab with the broken heater's knob.

Coins drip from your pockets like coils of wire, the bloom
        of *that empty treble roll* unfurling on the seasick floorboard

as you growl *I can afford awful. But, at least I can*
        afford it and mumble something about
the five stages of death as we slide into the parking space.

Recycling

The cans and the bottles you left
behind you wherever you went,
on our mother's porch with the sun falling,
telling my friends about the place across town.

Behind you wherever you went,
you left them empty and alone,
telling my friends about the place across town
where they paid two cents per can.

You left them, empty and alone.
You called us every mother's day.
Where they paid two cents per can,
you always had easy money.

You called us every mother's day.
My friends went to the community center
for some of that easy money.
Knee deep in that aluminum yarder,

my friends and I at the community center
scooping with trash cans we'd pilfered,
knee deep in that aluminum yarder,
filling the truck bed in the darkness.

Scooping with trash cans we'd pilfered,
the ringing brimmed our ears like water,
filling the truck bed in the darkness
like leaning scales we stood beside.

The ringing brimmed our ears like water,
on our mother's porch, with the sun falling
like leaning scales. We stood beside
the cans and the bottles you left.

Self-Portrait as Silent Ritual

I

When the feeling returns, it is time to circle the house
with senescent light caving out the kitchen window against
sharpening noon. Retrieve the blank parchment and toss
the top sheet as an offering to the air. As it flutters
toward the rug, think of synonyms for your regrets, blankness
glistening like a mantra, everything goes. Look out at the band
of jaybirds fighting over the cat food. Take out the cigar box
your father gave you for your tenth birthday where you keep
four quarters and a bag of salt. Place a pinch beneath your tongue
until it glows like silver and you unroll the negatives
which enshroud your inkwell, slowly from their dark axis.
Savor each frame light caresses. Take the quill
from your mother's coffee cup. Run your finger across
vines that move along the rim. Everything goes. It is enough.

II

Only in the empty room can you undress
                     the darkness with your eyes.

Riding through neighborhoods at dusk,
I am confronted by these late shadows:

this universe fashioned from curb to stucco,
                squares of grass blades, dying Bradford pear,

    the sweetgum lobbing its spherical spears

hiding their silence behind a covert of crisp leaf-piles,
                             a drowsy Lotus tree,

bent like the Buddha and as still.
                        Now you must burn your books
outside in the tin trash can, leaving
                   the shelves barren with dust.

Forget the photographs in the hall, but also focus inattention

on what may come, eat the fruit of unmindfulness to know
                        what matters most,
                                    what matters only

is the dirt beneath your fingernails.

                        III

All those times I felt I could know it, that it could be known,
I had misunderstood best. Not until dog days crouch
at Orion's feet, laying blame and scorching dry loam,
do I grow mad from sour wine. These narrow nights, when
for a moment, I see how time spreads itself like moss
over the rock's throat. In the enormous shade
of that magnolia we climbed, I remember—a word
which comes from memento—what is only a harbinger
carried in the mote of morning sunlight, thrumming
these ancient floorboards, threatening to reclaim
even them with caresses. Fading star, not unfolding
like dark blossoms out the window toward its symmetries,
instead you splinter in all directions at once. Is it enough
when every move leans toward this inevitable silence.

Emily Dickinson Sewed Her Poems Shut

Tight as lead caskets,
she locked the fascicle-box;
still, everyone reads them.

Plastic Realms

When the low pull of trainsong
     through the chain links
distorts the cloudless landscape

into folds of some tawdry skirt,
      shiftless and warm,
begging my eyes to touch the shapes

     of dying star and natal horizon
like some cold font on a yellowing map,

     worn down by the ways we had been folded
into new shapes by those giving directions

at gas stations. Annotations of exit ramps, where
     familiar pens had pressed their shapes

into the places now which pleaded
    as some dissipating fog over the bridge,

like that pillar of light,
     moving through the virgin haygrass
wild and abandoned detritus—

through the rubble and decay
   of flotsam after a long drought
had settled over the streets—the memory of a rain

where the river of darkness echoed, tearing loam,
    voices calling for our departure, homeward,
until the words of our lips were unintelligible,

      soundless against this broken sky,
and we could not find our way back
to the places from which we strayed.

Funeral Games

Imagine you were still
here, that you never left
your wife and your children
in the night, to cross eight
states for as many years.
Your daughter gallops onward
like a charioteer, but at the lake's
edge, your sons are still building
the fire, watching the bobber
drift, suspended between
the whiskey-dark surface and stiff
autumn air. They are boxing
your ears where you lie
as still as an old photograph,
scar visible on your forehead,
bottle spilled beside
the ring of rocks, draining
the dregs for that contest
already won. You told me
you were happiest at sixteen,
when the girls too good
to speak to you at school
would open their windows
slowly in the clean darkness.
This, too, will smolder
until morning comes
and I shake this miserable
dream, borrowed like a leaky
Jon boat from some silent
semaphore, keys to a house
long gone, locks changed,
the stucco now a shade
of robin's egg. The neighbors
moved and left behind
no forwarding address.

Threshing Floor

You cannot separate truth from chaff. Don't try it. Our minds
aren't near a ball of wax whose nail-sunk channels grow soft
when turned in warm palms. Instead, our thoughts propagate
like bloodroot, borne on the backs of fire-ants in the drainage ditch—
words lured by the odious ephemera of success, elaiosome
of autumn leaves and clouds moving across the night sky.
On wasted scraps of grocery lists, midden of misprints, & frass
of lines, it roots and forages the skull's ruined monuments.
It can't or won't explain the poem you forgot in the dark,
trading sleep for ink. Night moves like a winnow, darkly
through the mind, over those unsalted fields of Carthage,
unless the words march off our tongues in search of sugar.

Against Naming the Dead

Awake beside you with a head full of shadows,
unasked as worn questions
simmering in the darkness, not expecting
an answer which is only a promise
to try and name it which means to believe.
Where did they go? Why did they come
like a dark visitor in the unknown night?
Even when the sun rose and flooded
the room and I had dressed myself
in the raiments of cynicism and despair,
I pressed the unspoken beneath morning habits
until they weighed like silver daggers,
unnamable in the night sky
and belonged to you more than me.
You gave your stillness so willingly
like a long kiss, an answer to this madness
that I held close to my skin,
and we bowed into the silence all afternoon,
not knowing what we were listening for.

II

Amphora

We mold clay into a pot,
but it is the emptiness inside
that makes the vessel useful.
             —Daodejing

I
Before dark had settled upon the land,
there was a moment that could have been
understood just when the sun hung behind
the window glass, in the frame of green
pasture and endless pines washing like a river
over the low slung earth, down the deep bank,
until it disappeared beneath its own horizon.

Sometimes the mouth quivers as it reaches
for a word that isn't there, into the question
like grey pages advance or recede. Failing sun,
I am unsure if this is my face or my father's
at the window of this dim house filling with night.

II
At the table as night passes like a highway sound,
filling the glass stem between my fingers,
tracing the chip along the foot, hidden in the crest,
delicate and beautiful imperfection covered
by embellishment, sharp secret touch makes
the dark river tremble like honeysuckle breeze.
Outside the stars are shattered filaments, why can't we?

III
A crow's shadow moved across the field,
        the nothing outside a self—
outside the self, nothing

blending blades of grass
      with bird wings sculpted by warm
drafts, which is to say revocable marks

before the clay has fired
      and changed color,
vessel of immeasurable depth

neither substance nor innocence,
      body of land transformed,
dark mirror's insoluble presence

crumbling like an idle hour
      not touching the grass
to bare resentment or desire.

IV

Johnson said a young man should write pastorals,
not pretend to understand the sorrows of a real life.
His advice: leave elegies and epics to the old bards.
How could he? Night isn't reserved for the grey
and the bald. It has frequented my house, filling jars
we had hung in the trees to hold dark willed spirits
until the branches snapped from the weight that spring
you died and the river swelled until it burst
over the vanished bank, taking all it could make off with:
lawn chairs, plastic champagne flutes, a tire,
scrubbing away topsoil like some wild broom
strewing grocery bags on its way to the sea.

V

    Without a word for being there
      we hover over the earth
like ice cubes   along the rim
                  of night

      on a base bubbled
            with breath
                  of the dead

VI

Break the glass and free the breath it held
for over a century the ancients
used vessels to carry goods from field
to market, so we are born in vast cities
which contain us like jugs of wine
when the yeast grew, and bustled, and worked,
and filled the spaces, and gobbled the sugar
till it was gone, then settled—leaving
only lees and liquor to remember them.

VII

Night is water when I can move like a minnow
through the moonless sky, dodging little stones
in the current, which is to say the present,
or maybe better movement like the studs
in Orion's belt whose light began swimming
a thousand years ago and whose burning now might
come to some child hereafter, or perhaps it won't
reach us in time to be poured into the cup
of a human eye before the bottle breaks.

The Burden of Dumah

With the first warm hour of April,
how long, how long, and what of the night?

Luminous stench, spring's birth-breath,
unraveling the silence of the dead,

slack as a wet whip,
a buckeye-green garden hose.

Morning over the low hill
suffers like a tossed coin,

driving amber sunlight
through the window as deliberately

as a nail into the righteous,
quiet flesh of the angry washout.

Far off, impermanent in its empty age,
resting against the memory of its shadow,

a harrowed cedar, all knuckles and nubs,
lone, barefoot on the river bank

where the wind's breath lingers
like Lethe on the tongue,

grieving in its silent way
for the miserable unborn

journey, out into the faraway
fires of the horizon,

and what of the night? And what of the night?
Silence, the awful weight drags like ploughshares

though loam, running red with clay.
How long, how long, and what of the night?

Farmland fractured at such a distance
that the interstate slithers, smooth as darkness.

Swift invasions of mimosa blossom,
a vulture circles in a cloudless sky.

At the Planer

He has chosen the walnut
for its hardness or perhaps
because it has been aging
so long that it may be fed
into the hot teeth of the mill
for hours, the violent sound
scattering sawdust like details
left out of a story. Yes, perhaps
it is for the years this board sat
by the length of green hose, coiled
as a garden snake, which still
bears the rust marks from an exhaust
pipe, on a hill beside the dark house
where the terrible shadows fall,
or maybe it is only the table he
imagines hearing—the one dovetailed
and inlaid with bits of cherry
and sycamore, pressed by time
like fieldstones until the knots
resembled crown glass bull's eyes—
or perhaps it is nothing he hears
in the pained song the board makes
each time it passes through.

A Note from the Edomites

The house of silence is built on yesterday's ruin.

Nero Bathes in the Aqua Marcia

Long before he was said to sing
The Capture of Troy fiddleless, but perhaps
with cithara or lyre in hand,
from the palace roof, with the best view
to watch his city swallowed in flames,

burning like the roses of his pleasure gardens,
Nero floated in those blue waters,
at the mouth of the aqueduct.
Its pristine and sacred body, polluted
with the profanity of his flesh.

This is how his disease would be known
to the frightened and furious public,
long before the ecstasies of the private stage,
the lush vineyards of the Golden House,
this shallow dip into madness and excess

was all he could do to quench
the fires of illness and desire.
There at the shore, giving his body
slowly to the water's icy grip
to cease the raving of his heart.

Prayer for the Great Dog, Central Alabama

Beyond midnight, we move along the lake's rim
in the light of a moon so bright that shadows fall
around us everywhere. In such a spectral landscape,
any movement in the dark trees is green thunder.

Across the starry lake, mist rises in long wisps
and resembles white snakes climbing like angels
into the silent sky.

Far off, our house appears in the trees as if on fire
with bulb light, the orange glow offers its familiar
beacon. For a while, we stand afraid to interrupt
the silence which has swollen until it filled
the lake and the green hill and the dark trees.

The moon sits motionless in its exile.

All at once the yearlings are everywhere around us,
moving stiff as stalks in the wind. They seem
so unafraid to be standing among us as they move
up the hill in the wounded way that deer sometimes
bound through the trees.

I can believe in death, for just this moment.
It is enough now to stand as if we were only shadows
passing through darkness, as if we were only a dream
they had outgrown believing, or they
were the dream and we were the children
moving for cover through the cold winter night.

Incantation

Rain sizzle on the swollen pond
each droplet a lost word spilling
into some forgotten river underground
names of dead-tongued sound
disguised in the still movement
of figures retreating. Ascendant
shadows grow bold as they
retrieve their old dominion,
round the rim where night rises
like a curtain through the trees,
revealing the ancient sacrifice,
smothering unbroken shapes
in little rivulets, disappearing
into the crease of forsaken dark,
which vouchsafes nothing
that I must soon be knowing.

Jim Morrison Believed that the Right Words in the Right Order Could Kill You

Lying in the dark waters of that tub,
velvet drapes trimming the night
inside the golden facade
of the rue Beautreillis,
listening to the voices
drifting up from the Seine,
with the light already going
out of his dull eyes,
and another cigarette, perched
like the last link
of a short, broken circle
on his swollen belly, burning
like a candle lit at both ends, lies
the beardless shaman, with that deep,
death-rattle cough ringing
in his ears. Who knows
what he mumbled to himself?

I Am Singing Now While Rome Burns

We cannot console ourselves
with these tiny kingdoms of dawnlight.
The days are dust-colored windows
we must stare through, darkly.

These tiny kingdoms of dawnlight
burn the broken landscape.
We must stare through darkly
spiraling peacock plumes, the ones

that burn this broken landscape.
Like gasping fish, flopping through
spiraling peacock plumes, the ones
who survive will drown in escher seas.

Like gasping fish, flopping through
our hours like a ship on fire. Those
who survive will drown. In escher seas
we float on endless horizons,

our hours like a ship on fire. Those
days are dust, colored windows
we float on, endless horizons.
We cannot console ourselves.

Self-Portrait as Apollo and Dionysus

Far and away, of course,
there is also the sunlight,
raving over row after row
of the green and silver cotton,
curving the way power lines
climb the sweet whisper
of low hills, wondering
where they are headed
until they disappear like bees
into the violent distance,
and across the street,
as if they were brothers
fighting in the dust,
the yellow eroteme
of a backhoe screams
for the red Alabama clay to take it
into the nearing future where men
stand with hammers
and wires like maternity nurses
waiting to swaddle the naked field
in neon language,
glowing until it could forget
the barren hiss of the stars
and the time when the leaves
curl and drift into the soft grass
weightless as unwritten words
slurring off of the highway sound,
tugging at the land's
swollen body of minutes
until it opens like the silent
mouth of a god,
and far and away, of course,
there is also the night.

The Silent Thrush

When the echo returns
from the lake's rim,
shadows edging
in the darkness that is
neither morning nor night,
far beyond the mossy
bank of emptiness,
I'll drift
like the fledgling
who danced outside
my window
all that afternoon
and then flew on
not knowing
to where or when.

Throughout the Dismal Glade Our Bodies Shall Be Hung, Each on the Wild Thorn of His Wretched Shade

The dentist sees shadows
deep inside my tooth.
A bubble behind the metal filling
that she drilled so calmly
into my bone late last winter,
when the rain writhed
down the windows of her office,
the storm shaking the young
and barren maple back and forth,
and I clenched my fists as tightly
as I had at eight years old
in a practice across town,
with a similar window, overlooking
a pond filled with beautiful grey geese
that nested like harpies in the low banks,
and a room with posters on the ceiling,
where the man said over and over again,
"stop crying. I had a six-year-old
girl in here last week that didn't
even complain." And later,
in the parking lot, with the bright,
late-June heat sweltering that maple,
I am thinking about how the cavity
will have to be filled again
to stop those shadows
from growing long in the tooth.

A Mill at Sunset

Present in the spectacle of sundown
is the liquor of your forgetting. The earth
spins around the sun in the purple darkness
like a miller's stone, grinding against night.
What if this is Hell? What if the world just gets
hotter and more crowded until there is nothing
except for this suffering. In the *Inferno*, Dante
saw those who commit suicide turned into a bush
the harpies would feast on. At dusk, the crows
assemble their murder in the chinaberry down
along the rockfence. Once, I dreamt a shadow
lifted out of my body and that this was me dying.
I knew that this shadow had dwelled before
in other flesh, but I wasn't ready to leave.
I reached over to grab you, but your shadow
started coming out and I dropped it in fear.
As I fell back into my flesh, I realized that
the only real sin is despair, to relish it
until it feels as tepid as Seneca's bath water.
Perhaps we are all up here with the other
virtuous pagans as the silver rim of the lake
grows thick and the sun sinks, the slow filling
of the miller's pond in the dark.
Life is a kind of madness I ache from.

III

Middle of Nowhere, Five-Thirty

Now it is later than I could have imagined.

There are two shores and I keep wondering
        which is the world and which the void,
but both are water and everything is
night, hanging like shadows on the riverbank,
                resting like Narcissus
in their own reflections on the dark water.

Filled with this murkiness,
        a sycamore branch leans
into the shallows, either reaching or being pulled.
I am now nowhere here,
        and I keep trying to decide
if it is morning or night
but know it cannot be either.

Surely it is this emptiness before me,
        the sour taste of moss and forgetting
moving through me,
              filling my throat like riverwater,
or perhaps like a burial song
        until I must come out for air.

Here it is earlier than I can believe.

Break of Dawn

Catastrophes of sunlight on the bedspread,
                                making the unknown
known. Symmetrical synecdoche of silence, the sun
           returns to enlighten wasted landscapes

of forgotten night. A single crow alights between
the blinds upon the creosote neck of a utility pole.

The feast has always passed when we resume
                                these narratives of despair,

so we wall the casements of our regrets
            to stave away the summer swelter.

Nostos

It arrives with the dark syllables of thunder
                                      rattling the panes, motes of rainmist
and a longing to return
                to the summer we broke the ground open
with picks, smell of cedar in fresh loam,
                            and the baby chicks doomed
by the stare of our wild dog.

When it comes ripe as honeysuckle wine,
mesh jelly-bags in hand,
reeking of yeast and clover,
                              the mind circles like a buzzard
seeking carrion of old voices and faces,
rooms recall disappeared rooms, ground
once broken.

New ground. The soul must seek new earth
                                    to turn.

In the backyard, there is place enough
to drive posts into the earth and lay wire
where the jays will perch
                            and watch for ripening tomatoes

to glean before the clouds blow rain
across the hill in early May, flooding the bare
and barren to bury the dead.

Red Sky at Morning

Recessed dawnlight spreads its little wings,
                burning its way across boundaries
of pine horizon, through the cotton lint clouds,
                              filling the locust

outside our window, in our little garden,
            where the chard comes into view,
with the empty parking lot and the brown field,
    all brimming with the fading orange glow.
The nervous robins sound like old voices,
    crying to me out from some other place,
and my grief is as shallow as the coming day.

Field Grief

Late in the darkness
startled by the sound of what
could have been the bleating
of a young calf the one
my father bottle fed
after we found his mother
at the edge of the field
the hay leaning heavy
with flecks of blood
and the red clay too hard
to bear the paw prints
already the vultures
had assembled for their
wake in the pines
with the sun bending
weary at noon's stalk
her body growing ripe
as we dug the shallow pit
worn handles of the shovel
straining against the clay
with shadows from the field
moving into the treeline
we loaded the truck
and still later heading home
when we discovered
the fledgling owls living
in the oil can that hung
to the left of the cabin door
what little refuge we require.

One-Man Renga in Late June, Lee County

Outside, thunder boasts
an impotent rain. Who stood
amongst strawbriars

with shadows growing long and
the day smooth in its lateness?

Why ask with words what
this world is for? Recalling
the winter we left

the oven on to keep warm,
fed our bills into the mouth

of a woodstove, one
by one, watching them tremble
and darken, then burst.

It is I who have walked
through overgrown paspalum

in air so thick that
each breath filled me with dark dreams
of mossy water.

All the way up the path home,
twisted as those ruined hallways

where the dead open
like blue doors in the forest,
amber knobs you fear

turning. Past the garden gate,
with night falling everywhere

where we stood, screaming,
when it was all we could do
just to draw some heat

between us, after late shifts,
driving home in dark flurries.

At the high hilltop,
the bees have not disappeared
from the possumhaw.

Why do we ask with words when
the air is thick with their song?

Fig Tree

We stole eastward toward the wall
like reverse shadows moving for dawn,
early fall sheltered in deep layers of
canvas leaves, barefoot on the loamy mat,
gnarled roots tracing knotted limbs, this tree
my parents planted the day they knew.

What we held that day between our lips,
garbling like first words with the sweetness
that comes from so many years of sunlight,
we could taste the sap of time in
the fig juice dribbling down our chins.
We were made like children pressing
soft green flesh in our fingers, and in them,
we could taste the purple heat of stars.

Roundel on a Thursday Morning

The weft of despair and love—love and then despair,
    these entwined threads, this hand in glove,
like death dwells in the scarlet fire of your hair,
    weaving the weft of despair and love.

Around and back, like Penelope at her loom, I wove
    and tangled fingers in this auburn snare
of strands reflecting morning sun, this warp of

dread. The dull month staring into the winter air
    past where her breath bloomed and doves
gathered on the sill, watched and waited there,
    unweaving the weft of despair and love.

Self-Portrait at the Mouth of Summer

Tall spears of dark grass muttering
                in the sawmill tune of failure,
saying *nocturne* with the dark syllables
        falling like a curtain over the landscape,

undressing over the black hill
              where the sycamore burned
          auburn with sun-fall dread
                like fingers closing my throat.

Rot and refuse greening in the field's
                inescapable pithing roll,
summer's last gasps
                smother the night
into leaving's revelation,

all but the grass chokes in this pressing,
                until the buttons of the sky
come unsnapped with singing

the lives we forgot
                    to call this one forth.

The way light pursues the darkness

like a rabbit moving through the field,
              silent into the autistic night.

Silent into the autistic night
              like a rabbit moving through the field
        the way light pursues the darkness.

To call this one forth,
      the lives we forgot
come unsnapped with singing

until the buttons of the sky,
        all but the grass, choke in this pressing
into leaving's revelation.

    Smother the night.

Summer's last gasps,
        inescapable pithing roll,
rot and refuse greening in the fields
like fingers closing my throat,

        auburn with sun-fall dread.

Where the sycamore burned,
        undressing over the black hill,
falling like a curtain over the landscape

saying nocturne with the dark syllables
        in the sawmill tune of failure,
tall spears of dark grass, muttering.

Sunfall Triolet

The tree undressed when she approached.
Down the long path, the birds gathered
before the fires of autumn encroached
and undressed the tree. When she approached,
the branch lay bare. Having lost the broach
of green chatter and bathed in silver and azure,
the tree undressed. When she approached,
down the long path, the birds gathered.

The Campfire

We went into the woods to build fires,
the way our fathers had shown us,
gathering twigs to burn like
small effigies we built of ourselves.

The way our fathers had shown us,
we gathered the slack and the day jobs.
To build effigies out of ourselves, we took
dance classes on Tuesday evenings.

We fell slack into the shitty work
and forgot to tell our wives about
dance class on Tuesday evening
(on purpose or out of despair).

We forgot to tell our wives about
the sharp pains we felt that afternoon.
On purpose or out of despair,
we packed the hatchback and drove off.

The sharp pains we felt that afternoon
did little to slow us on our course,
as we packed the hatchback and drove off
for the seclusion of gravel roads.

Though it did little to slow us on our course,
we thought about it as we passed
from pavement to gravel oblivion,
the slack and the agony of day jobs.

We thought about it as we passed,
gathering twigs to burn like
the slack and the agony of day jobs.
We went into the woods to build fires.

Nocturne in an Empty Field

Perhaps it could be day a while longer
in the raptured grass, burning orange
with melancholy, where you once stood,
watching your own son run down the treeline
with a throat full of fire and the forest
already filling with darkness
like a bowl spun out of the red clay paths
left where the cows sought water
and moved for shelter when silence fell
as rain does over the gentle give of the earth,
where we children sat back-to-back
in the moonless field, watching for shadows
stalking the wood's edge. This night
recalls nights fallen. Coming home
from college to find the cows all sold
and you having slipped almost behind
the dark curtain of senility but peeking out
to remember it was time to press against
the mud of the low place where the cattle ate,
where the loam hardened and kudzu flung
its shawl over the face of the green hill,
where you stood, recalling a cairn built
at the edge of the river as night softened.

At Six, I Prayed For Snow In Alabama

I saw angels in my uncle's chimney, below the mantle

that glowed like polished stones and could not understand
        the patience of the little mouse, safe in its stocking
stuffed into the single page of that cloth calendar
            which hung on the front door, all dally and delay,

but moving closer, in no hurry to see it through
        the end of that long-awaited day
where the distance between minute and minute
was filled with anticipation and dread.

Self-Portrait in a Broken Mirror

Driving out through the fields at dawn,
                      dry grass resembles the strofades
out along the bank where the cows wade
       in the shallow mud pits,

       and here, the glimmering past is just
a glimpse in the broken rear-view
             mirror of that Oldsmobile—
at sixteen, at twenty five,

       again at the field's edge, hangover
thrumming with engine hiss,

spring daylight pouring out like a darkling river,
moving from where I know not
out toward where I can only imagine.

                      Once it is gone, it is gone
at once into those cracked lines,
      where the light veers forward and away—
the wet odor of gardenias

in the oppressive summer heat—a memory eating its tail
and sunning itself like the copperhead
           that writhed along the gravel path, vanishing

beyond the shallow mud pits of the lime quarry
          I would deliver pizza to on Thursdays,

     where the ghostly-powdered ground
seemed to ask, *Perché mi schiante? Perché mi scerpi?*

There the cranes howled and the creeks
would turn the strangest color of blue,
though we would wade in anyway,

            drifting with the currents beyond the shallows—
                  out into the glimmering past
until evening threatens and herds us back
            like shadows onto those blue cloth seats
with their cigarette burns

and down the darkening highway
            out of the cold, clean air that smells
rich with cow shit and honeysuckle.

Rain Follows the Plow

That beautiful arrogance we've carried with us—
in the mad blooming of late spring,
awake at some impossible hour, with the moon
                burning like the first fire over the river—

this endless need to try and describe,
        to put it down like arching lines of seed,
the exhausted night, bending like a locust in the wind,
where the stars look shattered in their frozen distances.

Night Rendering

1

When night comes writhing
out from the thawed earth
like a ball of snakes in April
unmindful and moving in all
directions at once I will wait
alone as if shaking the same
desolate dream I have been
having all my life of seasons
turning threadbare as tires
toward the edge of town.

2

When night comes and fills
my ears like rain on the roof
of the cabin my father built
and poured his shadows in
the moss closing over the hill
where it has stood all my life
gathering night like stones
in the riverbed when there
is no moon we call it new
because it appears to us
only as an absence except
for faint traces in the sky.

3

When night comes I believe
only in the distance of stars
over these abandoned fields
gone wild to seed the hollow
oak that bowed in the ice storm
after two-hundred years
the one grandfather fell in
when he was trying to clean

leaves out to stave away the rot
and he hung there for hours
like a man trapped in a well
until my father found him
by chance just barely noticing
his legs flailing in the green branches.

4

When night comes I can hear
the past most clearly it is you
grandfather who walks among
the strawbriars and still trees
mending pasture fences in a night
with no moon which means
to say it is hidden in plain sight.

Futurist Author Egotists

At the gates there grows the *litchi*. Who or what to earth is the logic,
nomads of insight, of the night's domain?
The self is there, fleshiest ether. There's the flies! Aid the dirt
underneath. I said, "inherent truth is dead."
When in the garden, there is always this tree who
regrets handing the seaway sinners delicious red fruit.
To this outrage, the futurist author egotists recoiled
and hide. Perhaps night-serpents ripen, slither,
then wish in the shade.

Coyote Makes This World

1

The universe is made of two gods
forever at play: hunger and silence.

2

None who lived among the god's creation
were ever so hungry as Coyote where he sat
alone in a cluster of light at the edge of the sky.

3

The stars are our liaison with eternity,
but from such a distance they appear cold.

All wild things tethered to the soil know this,
and reach desperately for them.

4

Far away, at the edge of a pasture, the persimmon
bows, heavy with fruit.

5

Hollow as the eye of a twinkling needle,
threading branch and pasture and sky.

6

Possum is in the persimmon,
perched silently on a bending branch.

7

Coyote lingers. He loves persimmons.

8

There is no beginning or end,
only the two at play, only apocalypse.

9

Between hunter and prey, there is only this play:
what is hidden, what is revealed.

10

Skein of winter stars unraveling,
as if pulling two pieces of a story apart.

11

Coyote plots at the trunk of the tree, playing idyll.
He looks to Possum, "certainly you must miss your home,
the forest."

"How I ache for it," cries possum, "but can never return.
You see, the gods have ordered me to protect this tree
from hungry thieves and tricksters."

12

Coyote writes a poem about the glistening forest
and gives it to Possum. While Possum is reading,
he pushes the forest as far from the pasture as he can.

13

Divided domains, stretched like a mother's arms,
shuddering into the distant air.

14

From such a distance, the forest burns
with silence like the stars.

15

"Your words resonate with truth," Possum weeps,
"my home seems further than ever."

16

"Let me help you out then," grins coyote,
"I could write another poem about the glistening forest
and remind you of your home, but you see, I have
grown hungry from my long journey across the sky,
and I cannot write on an empty stomach."

Blackberry Winter

And we could not hide our astonishment
                         when it arrived, carrying threats
of those silver ice-beards the cars refused
                         to shave that long winter.
When summer's pastoral flavor was all we had wished for,

the dogwood burned in the green field
until April shed
                         the young grass' bucolic guise,
revealing the stiff amethyst brambles
                         like a reflection from that other world.

Notes

"The Broken Branch" responds to James Wright's poem "Two Hangovers," originally appearing in *The Branch Will Not Break* (1963).

The italicized words in "To the Liquor Store with Hayden Carruth" come from his book *Scrambled Eggs & Whiskey* (1996), first given to me by his grandson Robin Ward, who has been a lifelong friend and does web editing for Kudzu House.

The title for "Throughout the Dismal Glade Our Bodies Shall Be Hung, Each on the Wild Thorn of His Wretched Shade" comes from lines 110-111 from Canto XIII of the *Inferno*. This poem was composed after a trip to the dentist, who later claimed to have been discussing this very canto in a church reading group the day before my appointment.

"The Burden of Dumah" is a reference to Isaiah 21:11: "The burden of Dumah. He calleth to me out of Seir, Watchman, what of the night? Watchman, what of the night?"

"I Am Singing Now as Rome Burns" is a line from Richard Siken's poem "Snow and Dirty Rain," from his first book *Crush* (2005). The line "we must stare through, darkly" is a reference to 1 Corinthians 13:12 "for now we see through a glass, darkly."

"Self-Portrait in a Broken Mirror" responds to John Asberry's poetry collection *Self-Portrait in a Convex Mirror*. The italicized words are from Canto XII of Dante's *Inferno*.

Acknowledgements

Gracious thanks to the editors of the following publications in which poems in this book first appeared, some in earlier forms:

The Boiler Journal, "The Broken Branch."

Borderlands: Texas Poetry Review, "Sunfall Triolet" and "The Campfire."

Blue Lyra Review, "A Heron."

Buddhist Poetry Review, "The Silent Thrush," "On the Field of Cattle Bones," and "Prayer for the Great Dog: Central Alabama."

Café Review, "Field Grief."

Camas Magazine, "The Burden of Dumah."

Canary Magazine, "One-Man Renga in Late June, Lee County."

The Citron Review, "Jim Morrison Believed that the Right Words in the Right Order Could Kill You."

Cumberland River Review, "Nocturne in an Empty Field," and "Nostos."

The Fourth River, "Self-Portrait in a Broken Mirror."

Ginosko Literary Journal, "Fig Tree," "Amphora," "The Mill at Sunset," "Against Naming the Dead," "Night Rendering," "At the Planer."

The Greensboro Review, "Self-Portrait as Apollo and Dionysus"

Harpur Palate, "Fish Tale," "To the Liquor Store with Hayden Carruth," "Funeral Games," and "A Genealogy of Silence."

Hawaii Pacific Review, "Self-Portrait as Silent Ritual."

ISLE: Interdisciplnary Studies in Literature and the Environment, "Middle of Nowhere, Five-Thirty."

Painted Bride Quarterly, "The Bicycle."

Portland Review, "Morning Otology."

Saint Anne Review, "Ubi Sunt."

Southern Humanities Review, "Coyote Makes This World"

Tusculum Review, "Self-Portrait at the Mouth of Summer."

Thanks to Village Smith Press for including "I Am Singing as Rome Burns" in *Bright Illuminations: The Art of Margee Bright Ragland and the Words of Others*.

"The Campfire" was selected by Peter Kline and Brittany Perham for Auburn University's 2014-15 Robert Hughes Mount, Jr. Poetry Prize.

"Coyote Makes This World" was awarded first-place in the 2013 "Mad Poets Contest" by the F. Scott Fitzgerald Museum Association in Montgomery, Alabama.

"Fish Tale" was awarded second-place in the 2014 "Mad Poets Contest" by the F. Scott Fitzgerald Museum Association in Montgomery, Alabama. The poem was also nominated by the editors of *Harpur Palate* for the 2015 Pushcart Prize.

Endless gratitude is owed to my wife Jane for her generous support, keen advice, and patience in the process of compiling this collection.

Section I of this book is in memory of my older brother David, and section II is in honor of my younger brother Nicholas, who survives.

Section III is for my father the poet and for my grandfather the novelist, whose trips to the family farm in Chambers County, Alabama inspired many of these poems and who are both responsible for my literary upbringing.

Gracious thanks to friends, editors, and teachers; for those who read early versions of these poems; others who offered their support along the way; and for those who continue to inspire me: Lee Rozelle, Kimberly Wright, Jim Murphy, Peter Huggins, Erica Dawson, Cecily Parks, Jericho Brown, Stefan Forrester, Keetje Kuipers, Karen Beckwith, Charlie Sterchi, Dan Morris, Gail Entrekin, Karla Linn Merrifield, Aaron Alford, Miriam Clark, Robin Ward, Arthur Wilke, and many others.

Special thanks to Tina Tatum, without whom this book would have been impossible, and to Jane and the poets Jim Murphy and Peter Huggins for their guidance on the book's title.

About the Author

Reflections on the Dark Water is the second book of poetry by Madison Jones; the previous book is *Live at Lethe* (Sweatshoppe Publications, 2013). His poems have appeared in dozens of literary journals, including *Painted Bride Quarterly*, *Harpur Palate*, *Portland Review*, *Tampa Review*, *Canary*, and *Cumberland River Review*; they have received awards such as the Robert Hughes Mount, Jr. Poetry Prize and others. He has reviewed scholarship and creative works for *Valparaiso Poetry Review*, *The Journal*, *ISLE: Interdisciplinary Studies in Literature and the Environment*, and *Kenyon Review Online*, among others. He is founder and editor-in-chief of *Kudzu House Quarterly*, a 501(c)3 nonprofit literary journal and press devoted to the promotion of southern ecological writing. He received a master's in literature from Auburn University in 2014, and he is currently working on his PhD in rhetoric and composition as a Graduate School Fellow at the University of Florida, where he works with the *TRACE* journal and innovation initiative. His scholarly work includes co-editing the recent collection *Writing the Environment in Nineteenth-Century American Literature: The Ecological Awareness of Early Scribes of Nature*. For more information, visit his author's page at ecopoiesis.com.

www.ingramcontent.com/pod-product-compliance
Lightning Source LLC
Chambersburg PA
CBHW020623300426
44113CB00007B/758